TRIBUTE

TO AN UNKNOWN SOLDIER

Published by iSeebookz Publishing LLC   Lagrange Georgia
Book layout and cover design format: Sheldon Rolins & Priscilla Sodeke
ISBN: 978-0-9995869-0-7

Printed in the United States of America
November 2017

10 9 8 7 6 5 4 3 2 1
First Edition

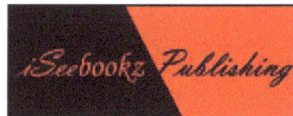

Dedicated To...

A Soldier whose footsteps are entrenched in the sands of time,

for every Infantry Earthling. Mrs. Eliza Bryant, my grandmother who had only a

third or fourth grade education, but a washpot full of Love, Wisdom and Understanding,

It was by her navigating abilities that kept me afloat as I traveled the rough seas of this life.

Mrs. Jonell Brockington of Conway, South Carolina, who encouraged me to remove this

work from the shelf collecting dust, and to my three children. A special thanks to Ms. Jackie Harper,

and Washington Street High School, Quitman Georgia.

Symbol Means: Tree of God-Altar
God's Presence and Protection

Tribute To An Unknown Soldier

By George Boston Rhynes

ISEEBOOKZ PUBLISHING LLC
LAGRANGE GEORGIA

TRIBUTE TO AN UNKNOWN SOLDIER

Amos 7:8 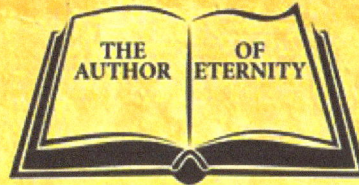 St. John 1:10

FOR CONSPICUOUS GALLANTRY AND INTREPIDITY
IN ACTION AT THE RISK OF HIS OWN LIFE ABOVE
AND BEYOND THE NORMAL CALL OF DUTY
SOMEWHERE IN THE MIDDLE EAST NEAR A PLACE
CALLED CALVARY

G.B.R.

A Soldier stepped out on the battlefield of time traveling from time into eternity, fighting with a sword called justice. At his birth insurgents were sent out to seek the unknown, and were met by wise men, who had been thoroughly-trained in all manner of military maneuvers such as

THE AUTHOR OF ETERNITY

espionage, sabotage and subversion, thereby being able to break every code of the enemy and maintain the secrecy of the mission. These wise men later operated under a "Shadow Commander", known at the time as a little child whose mission was code-named "Everlasting Life."

THE
AUTHOR OF
ETERNITY

On the battlefield of time he worked his way through the ranks, say forty-two generations, but was falsely accused and abused by the enemy, but because of his importunity, he continued to fight with the sword of justice. He told the commanding officer of the enemy forces how his life

THE AUTHOR OF ETERNITY

and that of his comrades could be saved, but they laughed him to scorn and said, "We have power to kill and let live." He allowed the enemy to carry him away captive, but he kept faith in his fellow comrades. Though captured and laughed to scorn, he never relinquished his weapons.

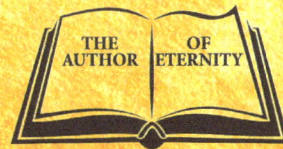

THE AUTHOR OF ETERNITY

When he arrived at the spot called "The place of the Skull", he stood bravely though surrounded by the enemy, and thought of the training he had received from his commanding officer, and he was not afraid. The enemy placed him on a platform and took his garments which

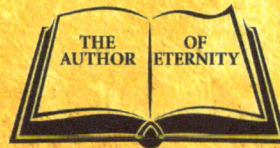

THE AUTHOR OF ETERNITY

consisted of a royal robe given him by his commanding officer. By mere strength, bravery, and some unknown "Ghost" to some, he withstood the pain of the nails being driven into his flesh. He was looked down on as a Soldier, accused of being a devil and degraded as a man. Yet he never

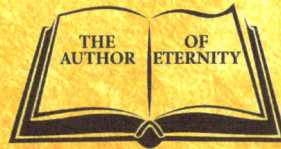

THE AUTHOR OF ETERNITY

deserted nor surrendered to the enemy. As he was suffering and dying, he yelled out to his Father, "Forgive them!" Then he bowed his head and gave up the "Ghost", and said, "It is finished." The man in charge of the execution wrote a title above his head in three different languages,

THE AUTHOR OF ETERNITY

Hebrew, Greek, and Latin, which may have been classified at the time but has since been downgraded for every one that will accept it. This great soldier was rejected, tortured, betrayed, lied on and brought to trial without a hearing, and sentenced to death for a crime he did not commit.

THE AUTHOR OF ETERNITY

Willingly he gave his life for the wrongs of the world, which was above and beyond the normal call of duty, but he never received the Medal of Honor. He was wounded many times but he never received a Purple Heart. He was the greatest pilot the world has ever known. He even flew himself into

THE AUTHOR OF ETERNITY

his father's house, and sat down on the right hand of the "Master Pilot", but he never received the Flying Cross. He was placed in a borrowed tomb, and arose on the third day, but we have omitted his name from among the world-renowned upon this planet.

He was a doctor, but we refused to make an appointment with him. He was a king, but instead of us giving him a crown of gold, we gave him a crown of thorns. He came through forty-two generations to abolish the sins of the world, yet he was rejected and despised by members of his own.

And as he hung on the platform of time,
we should have placed spices and gifts in his
hand; instead, we drove nails through his hand.
He walked more than seventy-two miles to
preach the gospel, and instead of us giving
him a new pair of shoes, we drove spikes
through his feet.

THE AUTHOR OF ETERNITY

He was a soldier that loved mankind, and after

his death we should have considered a

heart transplant, instead we pierced him through

his heart. This Great Soldier was not an electric

clock, but on the battlefield he kept

good time. He was not a nuclear bomb but his power was devastating. He was not the ring leader of "Watergate" but he spoke of a "Heavenly Gate." He was not the M.X. nor a Cruise Missile, but his love has cruised the world over. He was not sought out by the

vampire world, yet his blood

was good to the last drop. This brave, outstanding

Soldier lived as an angel, died as a thief and rose

to be the Mayor of mayors, Governor of

governors, President of presidents, Master of

masters, King of kings, and will be crowned Lord

of all. For his gallantry and heroic

action above and beyond the normal call of duty,

we never presented him with the Medal of

Honor, nor the Flying Cross, not even a Service

Medal. But today we as a people should

recognize him as the King of kings,

Master of masters, Supreme and Everlasting

comrade beyond the wisest man's comprehension,

and truly the son of God. For his ways were not

our ways, and his thoughts were not our thoughts.

No! There is no medal nor precious stone, we

can give a soldier of such Royal Value, but we can

pay tribute by living Holy before him, which is

our reasonable service. No end,

but one soon to come.

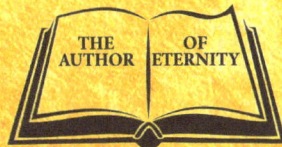

BIO OF AUTHOR

George Boston Rhynes born in south GA was reared by his grandparents Eliza and Howard Bryant. He is a minister and a retired military veteran who has traveled overseas to such places as Okinawa Japan, Germany, Guam, Thailand and many other countries. He is an author of several writings and has received recognition from many areas of the country. This is a special edition of Tribute to an unknown soldier in book form; its earliest edition was given as gifts to two US presidents and to several civil right leaders as a plaque. Mr. Rhynes still resides in South GA, however he is a traveler spending time with family and friends and helping others.

THE AUTHOR OF ETERNITY